Belief Systems

Belief Systems

Tamar Yoseloff

Nine
Arches
Press

Belief Systems
Tamar Yoseloff

ISBN: 978-1-913437-92-3
eISBN: 978-1-913437-93-0

First published June 2024 by:

Nine Arches Press
Unit 14, Sir Frank Whittle Business Centre,
Great Central Way, Rugby.
CV21 3XH
United Kingdom

www.ninearchespress.com

Printed in the United Kingdom by:
Imprint Digital

Nine Arches Press is supported using public funding
by Arts Council England.

Supported using public funding by
ARTS COUNCIL
ENGLAND

Contents

Combines

Ideas are one thing and what happens is another

– John Cage

New Year

Cloud veils houses and cars,
the drowsy street.

Tears hang from bare
branches, small offerings

for the season of fresh starts,
all those resolutions like cut pines
lined up for the bin men;

for poems struck through,
a thought nearly born before words
disintegrate, brittle petals.

The forecast is bitter.
Cracks in the pavement
are wide enough to fall into

and there will be no one
to lift you, just a crow
sounding his old alarm.

Blue Rag Zine

1.

a slack clock melts frost
ferns crust the skirting board

the country gathered in vagrancy
before the stooping waif

he sinks in centuries of bracken
a clockwork of hedgerows

deep blows
               he lives in
forgotten glades and gullies

grassy pirate hideouts
demands his own sun's century

footprints loosening time's edge

2.

morning ploughs brown furrows
in his mind
               distant silver moments
               half-wild with regret

he turns his back on man
slopes into the field
land tracked in secrecy

earth wears his touch
thorns each strut

his life numbered and shut

Field Companions

mestostics after John Cage

(isolation)

Only **i**n caves and houses
do we thrive, i**n** fretting circles
or bubbles, **w**e feed on
what we can f**o**rage, plants
and sl**o**wer creatures;
death arrives for
tho**s**e who can't adapt.

We dine on **m**ushrooms, pale
flesh flak**i**ng on our
lip**s**, their nutty vigour
nourishing our reso**l**ve. *We will fight*
someon**e** shouts, raising a fist
but **d**efeat is easier

bending into wind
like a yew in a grave**y**ard, its roots
clutching bones;
into rem**e**mbrance we dissolve
for p**a**rasites
and ner**v**ous violets,
not an **e**nd
ju**s**t another cycle.

Heartsease

Outside they run riot, sprout
where they can in the glare of noon;
they don't need tending or care,
don't care about us

when we're down on our luck,
little pansy faces giggling.
We demand they cure our ills,
stir thoughts of love –

enough of them, a fast death
once cut. Who wants to be
cooped up with their sweet reek,
their sentimental pose?

They live with or without
our passion, find their feast
in air, in the new-turned soil
on our graves.

Common

To walk here now
you'd think we'd given up:
all dried-out fern and brush,
knotted brambles
blackbird-stripped.

Little glots of bullace
pucker on the tree,
choice fruits lace its canopy
just beyond our reach.

Prints of dogs and hooves,
our heavy-soled shoes,
pressed in sand until the first
stiff wind – how simply
we lift from earth.

Witch Touch

Our lives should go between the lichen and the bark. The eye may see
for the hand, but not for the mind. We are still being born, and have
as yet but a dim vision of sea and land, sun, moon, and stars . . .
  — Henry David Thoreau

A stain of life
clasping brick in this park
edged by traffic.

Tough growth,
flourishing unnoticed
as it fruits: it will live out

land grabs, viruses, wars,
its sharp constellations
spreading

*

No one comes here anymore,
not in a month of Sundays.
I'm wearing that yellow dress,
my hair matted with twigs
from the place where we lay
in the long grass under the yews.

You are a stone dog keeping vigil
for its owner, hoarding secrets,
your limbs stiff with devils' claws,
your ears stuffed with trumpets.
I try to say your name but my mouth
is sprouting primrose.

*

You are in a wood, conifer and spruce
fencing sky. Deep inside the thicket

trumpet cups of *Cladonia fimbriata*
raise their bells to blast still air.

Only the deer can hear them,
can feel your breath sough the leaves.

Summer Fields

I very often find I'll take my paints to a certain place that has moved me and I'll begin to paint there and I find perhaps by the end of the summer I haven't moved from that place – my paintings are still there and I've worn a kind of mark in the ground . . .
  — Joan Eardley

In the margin of land the farmer left unsown
cornflowers and daisies stake their ground,
alert heads raised to sun. This is the place
between wheat and wild where I will stand,
grass sticking to canvas, boots planted in dirt.
The sun is making gold of plain old hay,
and all I must do is make my mark, my hand
understanding what the mind can't grasp.

Glory be to field, to sun, to the harvest
that will feed the farmer, his brood, this village
and the next. But I must also paint the storm
that shades the sky, lifts a chill that breathes
little whispers on my skin – a sign
it's time to say goodbye to easy days.

Half Life

The ones before us passed this way,
each step clogged in mud.

Now they're gone, the path
pocked with tracks, hardened

casts of ghosts. We skulk through
lanes and glades, keeping

our distance; distance is all we've got,
the space around us haloed

but we're not angels. We lock ourselves
in attics, crazy Berthas

crying to the moon, no one
around to hear. The streets rewild –

creatures come out of hiding
while we retreat, our ragged secrets

stuck in struts of junked machines.
What we've learned of truth and trust

isn't enough. There's a shadow
we can crawl into, not come out.

Field Companions

(magic)

Alice placed
a golden teacher on my tongue
and we drifted outside to find ghosts
                    diving through trees,
like clouds, but with skeletons. The air was
a room we could enter. Everything
                    had edges.

There was a line I kept reciting about
coffins and keyholes, the more I said it
                    the more I wanted both.
          Alice said once you arrived you had to stay;
we were in a garden in Paris –

I don't know how we got there, how we returned
          but suddenly it was morning

and everything was grey. For years after
          the ghosts materialised,
                    mostly when I was empty.
They'd appear when night was
          at its blackest, in the hinge
between night and day; they'd come
to tell me that death is like
          a river you ease yourself into,
after the first terrible plunge

          it's fine, almost like being
          alive, except you've abandoned
          your body –
it has no purpose anymore,
                    its ponderous limbs and vexing organs
gone – and you're reduced to vapour,
          a pure wind.

Bridges

A bridge to me is beautiful. I like the idea of getting from one side to the other
 – Joan Mitchell

I miss them – their clear reach across the river,
and me, on foot, on the top deck of a bus,
water watching, the Thames still and dull
even in sun, and I think of the mudlark sifting
gold stuck in sludge, a thousand losses
washed up with the tide; I think of my student
who threw herself off Lambeth Bridge one night,
passport in her pocket, always considerate,
knowing the coroner would be needing it;
I think of frost fairs, river solid enough
to clone its city on ice, and pleasure boats,
Dutch barges decked with pots of cranesbill;
I think of death undoing Friday crowds
on London Bridge, the boys who drove
a hired van straight into the thick.
I miss all those strangers, our city shut up
like an oyster worrying its pearl,
as I stick to my grid, never venturing
far enough to find the river's glint –
all that mighty heart, as the poet said,
stopped, the monitor switched off.

Night held

at bay by the stuttering strip light,
rectangular god
            of the arctic garage.

Once there was industry,

something happening,
something you could believe in –

now steel has grown sullen, throws
phantoms in corners.

Sun was a fact once, a promise –
but it can't reach here

where chill is reptile,
            chill is a coat you can never shed.

You're caught in this sleepless zone,
            in this sodium glare,

your heartbeat in sync
to the drip of the tap,

lost drone of stopped machines
trapped
            in stilled air.

Coyote in the Suburbs

for Susan Tomlinson

Once an artist caged himself
with one of their kind;
at first they circled each other,

pressing limbs into corners,
backs into wire, discovering
the shape of confinement:

the coyote was not tamed,
but came to know the artist
as skin and blood, understood

how each movement was a kind
of reckoning – prisoners together.
The artist was making a stand

against a foreign war, a nation
cleaved by boundaries; the coyote
was its own stand, stubborn

wildness, defying what we suppress.
We retreat to aircon rooms
while they advance into yards,

our swing sets and teak chairs
fenced by clipped privet too neat
to hold their jittery bones.

We want to venture to the edge, into
uncharted lands, reach out our hands
as the artist did, touch coarse fur.

Chirophobia

The hands that come for me are gloved
and white, like a butler or a clown –
I could be served or slapped.

They spider up the walls, hover over my head –
bony birds, portents of death.
They aren't real, but I can see them.

I've been in this room for months,
maybe years; my ribs are lath and plaster.
The hands know I'm done for, each finger

has a mind of its own: the first is dictator,
the fourth is speaker, the thumb
is a club to beat me dumb.

The hands sit across from each other
at my table and drum, drum, drum.

The Killer's Hands

In slasher flicks there's often a close-up
of the killer's hands. Stranglers have meaty palms
slippery with sweat.

Stabbers are svelte-wristed,
with long bony fingers; sometimes they don
black leather gloves so they don't leave prints.

People say *I could kill him with my bare hands*
but it takes great strength, steely nerve.
It helps to be insane.

In slasher flicks it's the girls in short skirts
tripping into night without fear
who are seen off first, despite their shrill screams.

The killer is often misunderstood. He kills
for love or company, or because he misses his mother,
was abused by his father.

We never learn anything about the girls.

Close-up of a bright blue eye, smudged mascara,
open forever.

Ignition

after *Things I did that nobody noticed (but that changed everything)*
by Sara Haq

The small blue flame
like a pilot light –

germ of hurt
sown in my heart;
with each blown breath

it grows, feeds
on my blood.

*

The small blue flame
of Zippo consumes

photographs, poems,
devours what I own,
incinerating memory;

your name still
scalds my tongue.

*

The small blue flame
rasps and frets – shy girl

trapped in glass, head
in the phlox, clouds
in her eyes. It must stop,

this weepy droop –
life is tough.

*

The small blue flame
spits spirits into air;

those with faith
can see them – bright
heads haloed –

those without know
how fire hates.

*

The small blue flame
of bruise; beneath

the skim of skin,
blood pools. A button
to press for pain

but this will fade
with time. Like new.

*

The small blue flame
tricks me to its core;

in the blaze, nothing
spared, all things
equal when cinder,

all things precious
smoulder to ash.

*

The small blue flame
nearest to the candle,

hotter than white;
its light slits the dark,
it makes a little sigh,

it loves my misery
alone at night.

Night opened in me an inn for phantoms

where the vampire from the silent film
pitched his shadow over the wall.

He ascended the stairs hands first,
the pull of moon stretching his bony fingers

like an old wives' tale longer longer.
I didn't believe in ghosts

but everyone in the movie was dead,
their faces infused with silver

and the actor became a vampire
in real life, or so they said, his terrible face

glued to my eyes. But it was his hands
that got me, his hands creeping along the wall,

even though I knew the shadows
were cast by headlights from passing cars.

I was an old soul in a child's body,
my nightmares dusty, like the things

you find in attics, desolate, passed over,
refusing to be brought to light.

Nothing exists that is forever

i.m. Christo Vladimirov Javacheff (1935–2020)

He started small, with cases and cans
trussed like frantic bundles people make
when forced to leave in the night
with what they can carry on their backs;
then cars, buildings, bridges, islands –
stamped with foot falls and thumbprints,
hammer blows and bullet holes –
shrouded like grave goods to be shipped
to the next world, no fixed address.
But he believed in this world,
what we choose to protect. To cloak
is to keep safe, as you would a swaddled child
handed to its mother like a gift. His gift
to us: our world under cover, hushed.

Fault Lines

When it fell –

white porcelain
blue and orange flowers
gold rim
Chinese
nineteenth century
maybe older

an object that survived
rough journeys
outlived
countless owners

until it was trusted to me
and slipped
through tired fingers
to the hard wood floor –

it shattered
into jagged pieces

you said *we can mend it*
so we will make a start

learning to live
with what is fractured.

Combines

I consider the text of a newspaper, the detail of a photograph, the stitch in a baseball, and the filament in a light bulb as fundamental to the painting as brush stroke or enamel drip of paint. In the end, what one sees as my work is what I choose to make with no guarantee of enlightenment, humor, beauty or art.

– Robert Rauschenberg, 1956

Canyon

If the artist wasn't dead already he could be
arrested for causing harm to a bird
under Federal Protection, although he claimed

the golden eagle suspended from the canvas
was shot and stuffed by a Rough Rider,
one of Roosevelt's 'cowboy cavalry'

named after Buffalo Bill's Wild West show
so maybe it's OK for a man to kill an eagle
if he's already a hero. The bird doesn't give a shit:

it resides with a postcard of Lady Liberty,
a torn white shirt, a metal drum, a squeezed-out
tube of paint, a b/w snap of the artist's son

and let's face it, the eagle is more famous dead –
not just a portrait of, but the real thing
in full wing. It never has to die again.

Rhyme

Where's the artist? He's disappeared
in the blinding white of another year

like the dancer who chanced across the stage
in a geodome of constant change

with a song that syphoned sound from air
and held together disrepair

to the lover who unfurled his flag
in a studio strewn with scraps and rags

now all that's left is a thrift-store tie
the kind that says he's a regular guy

but you wouldn't catch him dead in that
just like those khaki boys sent back

stitched up in their uniforms
who thought that faith could stave off harm

but the artist has no truck with gospel
he calculates the great impossible

how to mend the busted earth
with the fragments of our wealth

Hymnal

It's gruelling to be wanted – the desirer's eyes
all over you, his lips mouthing your name
like a benediction. His love is a prison, or a room
with flocked wallpaper where a mad aunt
sleeps, her dreams fettered by demons.

The desirer carves your name in trees and walls,
letters trapped in love hearts pierced
by feathered arrows. You no longer recognise it
or come when called. You never owned it,
only a name, shared with strangers

pressed into those thin White Pages,
like Frank and Bill and Jack – manly names
that pack a punch, American names
with ten-gallon hats and loaded guns.

Monogram

Only a heel could pass him by,
with his loveable beard, his hangdog eyes –
a god of sorts, not the devil
the gospel said, certainly not a communist

although he always sat to the left.
It's tough to be daubed with the sins
of the world, saddled with that spare tire,
the junk of the century at his dainty hooves.

Eventually we all get put out to pasture
no matter how useful we were, how loved;
born to decline, the way a new car
tanks in dollars as you drive off the lot.

This is his lot – schmuck, sucker, fall guy –
he'll never be on top, never know
what it's like to be truly prized. It's no ball
being him. It really gets his goat.

Bed

Things get messy under the sheets,
the squelch and spill of love. The artist
fucks his way cross-continent, taking in
the sights: Old Masters with ass and tits.
The Grand Tour, sighs with Cy, the finger
of a Colossus pointing North. But South
is where they head, to the Med, gentle
gentian sea. A game of hide and seek.

Things get messy. Boys and girls
tumbling in Aluma Black, clits and cocks
and who knows what. The carnal clock
is ticking. Soon he will enter the world
feet first, rubbing sleep from his eyes.
He's made his bed. Now he must lie.

Factum

Time is the mirror lake: what really happened
and what you remember. Two trees as tall
as each other, and through them you can see
to the opposite shore. You have been rowing
for many years, even when it seemed as if
you were still. Now you're in a room
where numbers crowd together on a wall:
the day you were born is marked in red,
the day you die it will be up to others
to light a candle. The photo captures your face –
the man at the border squints and looks again.

Look again. The man at the border squints.
Light a candle. You're captured behind your face
until the day you die, then it's up to others
to mark the day you were born in red.
Numbers crowd together on a wall;
you're still in that room, where you've been
for many years. Even then it seemed as if
the opposite shore could be reached by rowing,
stretching farther until you could see
two trees as tall as you remembered.
What really happened? The mirror lake is time.

Trophy I (for Merce Cunningham)

His stride clear as a bell, he tilts
to the whim of gravity, arms out-
stretched to hold air – invisible
partner, Ginger to his Fred. Easy
as falling off a horse, to dance
while the world stops short but
still he keeps spinning like a top
trips the gap in the boards, bored
with *pas de chat*, that old hat
he wants to doff, like Isadora's
scarf, throwing caution to wind
and prudence in the bin. This
is where we begin, with baby
steps, a glissade to the left and
then straight into space, where
the stars form a map of time
a new routine, each footfall another great leap into the dark

Trophy IV (for John Cage)

The composer knows that beauty is
everywhere, even underfoot. He tunes
his antennae to spores lifting from earth,
to city streets that offer gifts, odds
and ends; if you know where to look,
one man's trash is another man's gold.

The artist beams a light on what is,
not what might be. A picture is like a tyre,
flattening space and time onto surface.
A stroke of paint means nothing much
but a boot speaks of endless journeys,
brute force, all those eternal tropes.

The composer gets a kick out of the artist
striking a blow for rag and bone.

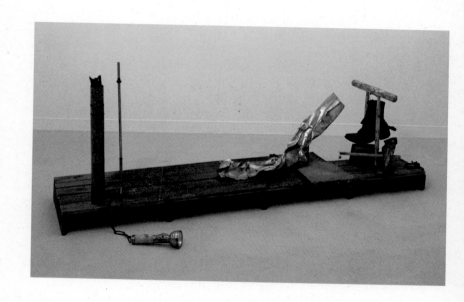

Levee

I brood inside my boudoir, skin like
a chalk cross on the plague house door.
This is the grave talking, where I've been
holed up, feels like years. Once I was in
the pink, but all flesh stinks when it goes bad,
king and clown alike.
                              If it keeps on rainin,
levee's goin to break, says the ol blues tune,
been raining all afternoon, and no let up.
A fine day for suicide, in my Sunday suit,
fancy tie my handy noose, if I wasn't lately
expired. No light through the trees,
just more damn trees.
                              There's always work
for the cold cook, whistling while he digs
that ol blues tune, *when the levee breaks,*
mama, you got to move, that's what he sings,
loud and clear from the field of bones,
thinkin bout my baby and my happy home.
But the light's gone out.
                              No body's home.

Trophy V (for Jasper Johns)

A picture is more like the real world
when it's made out of the real world

so I can't paint your portrait, fix
your face to canvas when you exist

in endless motion like Duchamp's nude,
descending the stairs in twos,

all lean limbs, my heart the target you hit.
I turn our bed on its side and call it art,

I blaze a trail across your skin
and claim my gift.

Through the glass the critics demand
your public stance,

the clean-cut white-shirt deep-south kid,
but I'm the jester to your jasper, the kidder

to your straight man, you are the silence
in the rowdy city of my mind.

You dreamed of the stars
and stripes, but your grab-bag flag stands

for this room, this minute,
the state we inhabit,

surrounded by all the things men break
which we make whole.

Summerstorm

The past is unzipped, like the backseat lover
loosening your tie. You were crazy about him
in June, sleeping past noon in the grass,
singing all night out of tune. By September
he'd split, without so much as a goodbye kiss.
It's tough to be the one who's ditched,
the scrub who gets bumped from the nest.

Now you're adrift in the city, its brick piles
blotting out sky; you're not fit for this life,
the sulky drama of the street. You want to kill
the taste on your tongue; green fairy, bitter pill,
whatever gets you by. Clouds mass
as the curtain rises on the last act,
you know already how it ends.

Painting with Grey Wing

No more flights of fancy
now you're trussed like a Christmas turkey,
grounded in a city that turns
on a dime, changes tack on a whim.

You thought you were one of the old gods,
plucking love out of air, but now
a cold wind howls; you must hunker down,
hibernate.

When you wake, the old gods will be dead,
young turks will rule the world.
They'll reinvent the wheel and call it art,
all paint-by-numbers stuff.

They'll have their day, as you had yours,
when music was clear as vodka
and everybody loved you, at least
that's what they said. Love –

in that frail instant, gone. Those boys
with their fair hair and paint-smeared shirts,
they were so beautiful, flying close
to the sun. You hear their voices

still, but the words are strained,
like a radio stuck between stations.
What can heaven mean, the poet asked.
You have no reply, you

who always had a ready answer.
Nothing to say that hasn't been said before,
no magnum opus about truth and beauty,
just a dead bird pinned to a board.

Field Companions

(time)

The present is
a needle stuck
on vinyl
ploughing the same groove again
and again –
a refrain
caught in space

I cite the past,
my silent pieces –

ghosts diving at night,
the musty spoors of the forest,
my legs white as stipes

quietly stretching in darkness;
nothing lasts
but in the mind, and the mind
can lose itself in brambles,

in passive revolutions –
old songs
occupy my ears,
the final chord
fades, but in my bones
I hold its sound.

In Memory

My quietness has a man in it, he is transparent
and he carries me quietly, like a gondola, through the streets.
He has several likenesses, like stars and years, like numerals.
– Frank O'Hara, 'In Memory of My Feelings'

If all the numbers were piled on top of each other
like they are in Jasper Johns's paintings
maybe we could stop counting.

Maybe he knew – and still knows, now he's ninety –
how days begin to merge into one
when you have lived a long while

and how the same events occur over and over –
catastrophes that alter the world,
become history, until they occur again

and suddenly you're living 'in extraordinary times'
even though you feel average, and wonder
how such disasters could happen in your life.

Johns painted *things the mind already knows*,
numbers and flags and targets,
to remind us what they stand for:

like the American flag,
sometimes whitewashed, a ghost standard
flying for an imagined country;

sometimes with newspapers
emerging under layers of acrylic,
like the ruins of fallen empires.

In his painting 'In Memory of My Feelings'
maybe he is thinking of his friend,
Frank O'Hara, who wrote a poem with that title:

it's stencilled at the bottom of the canvas,
then the words A DEAD MAN.
O'Hara would die five years later

in a freak accident on Fire Island,
the kind of death no one expects at forty,
a number we think of as 'mid-life'.

Johns traced a skull in the top right corner,
then painted it over, but it's visible
with infrared technology

like in A&E when the doctor displays your X-ray
and you remember this is all you are:
just bones scaffolding skin.

My quietness has a man in it,
O'Hara wrote, and now and then you realise
you're more than bones and skin; you have dreams

you conceal beneath the surface.
Like Johns's secret skull, still present, lurking
under a sea of grey; while the artist,

a young man, a silvery star, carries himself
through streets, then years, and keeps painting
to stop himself from counting.

25th February 1970

Rothko took off his glasses
and the studio clouded over,
removed his shoes, his trousers

but kept his socks on,
the kind executives wear,
fine knit, black.

> In the street
> men hailed cabs, black
> patent shoes refracting light.

> Ice cracked as they clinked
> highballs by the pool
> at the Four Seasons.

The murals devoured him,
demons steering every stroke,
black on maroon.

> They lived for the cut and thrust.

He slit his right arm,
one razor-straight line,
maroon on white.

> Hostile takeovers, blood sports.

He was found in a pool of blood
six by eight feet wide.

The painter in his prime

i.m. Léon Spilliaert, 1881 – 1946
(for Sean O'Brien)

The painter has been dead more years
than he lived, which suits his disposition;
he found the corpse within when young

and carried it through brooding boulevards
until it was dark enough to begin
then he climbed inside the night,

the city his sick bed, its patients turned out
to wander under sulphurous lamps,
mourners at their own wakes.

A couple of wars, an epidemic; he's seen it all,
his bulbous eye like a periscope
rising from a dim sea.

The Sea, No. 4

i.m. Joan Eardley

It's late when you walk out,
sky blotched by an anaemic moon,

the sea so cold it passes through you
like a knife. You enter the house

to find the canvas waiting, that darkness
brought inside. You hold it in your body.

For all these years you keep returning
to the painting, adding the chaos of waves,

wan moon lighting their milky longing
as they stretch thin over the shore.

Late they say in the catalogue
describing the finished painting, now hanging

in a private collection – a private moment
between you and sea and night

when you must have known you were ill
and maybe wondered

if you'd have enough time to complete
one last seascape. This life's work

never finished, the sea insisting,
retreating, and your body insisting,

retreating, the way cloud throws
a veil over moon.

Right After

i.m. Eva Hesse

Right after her operation she came back to her studio
with her head bandaged in gauze
like a dead Egyptian princess.
She was working in fibreglass, and loved
how it arrived in long bands, strings of pearls
she dampened in resin then draped from the ceiling.

Right after she made it, she knew she was on to something,
but didn't live long enough to see where it would take her.
Right after she died, her friend talked about seeing her
with those bandages around her head,
a runnel of blood on her cheek.
She would have thought that was beautiful.

Right after the war she'd come to New York with her family.
They managed to escape, but years later
her mother jumped out of a window.
It was difficult to be a survivor.

Right after Tom left, she took off her wedding ring.
The same year her father died.
All that loss.

Right after she came out of hospital
she started working again, several sculptures on the go,
never enough hours in the day.
She worried the work wouldn't last, it would break,
wear badly. She could never get it right.

She named the final piece *Right After*
as if it was poised on the verge of something more,
loops of time suspended in the gallery
and you couldn't see the wires that held it.

Suite for Two in Space and Time

This is where they meet, in the gap between backs –
one body unarching, bringing the other

draped across him like a cape
to his feet, so both are standing but not facing.

Please kiss whatever part of you
you can reach for me Cage wrote to Merce

and Merce could reach many places, his body bending
space, his lasso limbs catching light.

They meet at the point of chance,
measuring breath in relation to the air between them;

the ball of a body unfurling is beautiful.
A body lying still is too

although even in rest, breath
is rising and falling. *I'm looking forward*

to seeing you again rather than backward
to having seen you recently Cage wrote to Merce

and their lives rewind, bodies held in pose
on a spotlit stage.

Words can't stand in for the act of looking
in a mirror where the other was once reflected;

I'm unsentimental Cage wrote to Merce
but really he wasn't.

Tacet

*It will open with a single idea which I will attempt to make
as seductive as the color and shape and fragrance of a flower.*
– John Cage, considering his lecture on silence

He wanted us to hear the sound of our own
breathing, the pin-drop quiet, the vacuum
we typically fill with muzak, endless voices
urging us away from the toughness of alone.

There's no place we don't occupy without
our buzz and rumble: stop, he tells us,
stop

                              and let silence come
like a roar, the longest sigh that stretches
beyond words; he knew there's no such thing
as an empty space, even when we're gone:

what we leave is out of sight, but clear,
splitting air with something without meaning,
at least not in language, and when it stops
we still hear it inside our bodies. It never stops.

Field Companions

(music)

I have come to the conclusion that much can
        be learned about music by devoting
           oneself to the mushroom —

acoustic **p**ad of the forest:
        p**l**ace your ear to the ground
    to he**a**r earth reverberating
in the long deca**y** before silence.

        Y**o**ur upturned ear tunes
    to the trees' **f**requency,
        a gu**s**t conducting branch and leaf.
    This is **h**ow to listen:
    slow rele**a**se from the clatter of world
    and min**d**
        c**o**rrupting the air
with the din of **w**hite noise.

Noise: A Lecture

/nɔɪz/

Noun: a sound, especially one that is loud or unpleasant

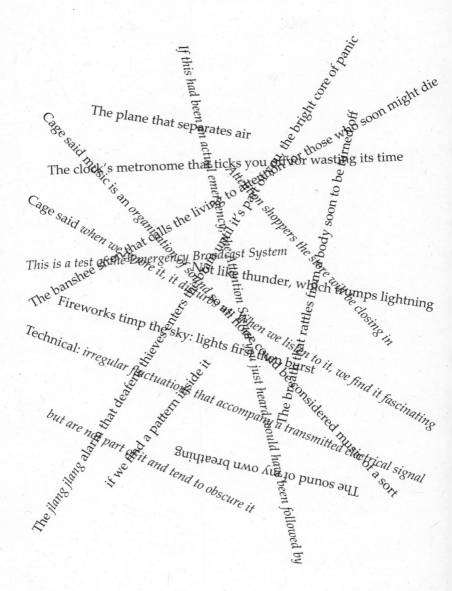

If this had been an actual emergency

the bright core of panic

The plane that separates air

Cage said music is an organized

for those who soon might die

The clock's metronome that ticks you off for wasting its time

Attention shoppers the store will be closing in

the body soon to be burned off

Cage said when we

Emergency Broadcast System

This is a test of the

Not like thunder, which thumps lightning

The banshee came before it, it disturbs all those

When we listen to it, we find it fascinating

Fireworks timp the sky: lights first that just heard

loud burst

The breath that rattles from

considered musical

electrical signal

of a sort

Technical: irregular fluctuations

that accompany a transmitted

would have been followed by

but are not part of it and tend to obscure it

The jlang jlang alarm that deafens

if we find a pattern inside it

The sound of my own breathing

69

In Concert

We were sitting in a crowded hall, waiting
for the lights to dim – before the halls
were emptied – strangers sharing breath,
breathing as one when the music began.
How strange to be silent together, listening
as sound filled the air; shallow breathing
of a man next to me, deep in concentration,
his arm against mine, the intimacy of listening
in the dark as time collapsed, his breath in time
with the music. I miss the brush of his arm –
it annoyed me then – I miss his breathing,
held on a note, waiting for the orchestra to rise;
liquid longing of the strings, the drums
gathering force, the horns' flash and fade.
The bare arms of the violins working as one,
girls in black, lifting the tune from the score.
Music could be conjured by a baton's wave
and we were its conductors, our bodies
pliant in plush seats, absorbing vibration;
all we had to do was allow it to enter.

Weathers

i.m. Imogen Holst

I arrive in her garden on the cusp of autumn,
held in the still breath of heat, the old apple tree

clasping its fruit in knuckled branches –
I admire their tenacity, those shrivelled globes

sucked dry by worms and wasps
hanging on for dear life – for life is dear –

I find the last good one before the drop
and pick it, slice into unblemished flesh;

it spoils before my eyes, what's inside browning
as it meets the air, even while the skin still glows.

She's gone, but the mantel keeps her face
in black and white. Her house settles

in its ground, her body long ago
broken down by busy earth.

This tree that sang to its roots with her notes
gathers itself for hard winter.

Belief Systems

We are absolutely committed to not knowing.
An act of faith it was once called. We put up a guess.
– John Latham

The storm is here. They give him a name.
The wild winds weep, we stiffen our limbs
to a winter with small consolation.
The night cloaks men in ceremonial duvets,
winding sheets, their beards entwining
as they sleep. They might have been
bards or kings *fallen on hard times*,
that's what they say, as if time
has surface, a rigid ground
that breaks the body as it hits.

Only events can fling us from our beds.
Events goosestep over concrete.
Events purge words of power,
the gutter press pressed thin against
windows to buffer wind.
                                Old news –
over before it's ink. We can only guess
what's next. An act of faith.

*

We take to the virtual streets, waving
emoji fists. The revolution is on our phone,
the event inside our pocket.

Hours of folly are measured on Facebook,
where poomogis run for president,
the dead update their status;

we tell the cloud our secrets
so it will hold our voices
when we lose solid shape:

nothing we've made will save us
from what we've razed. When the foaming
flood hits shore
                    our time is up.

*

The storm collects our waste.
Circuits bared, maps to nowhere.
Analog screens, their ancient stars
trapped in static. All of it shipped
to Surabaya; farmers ditch failed crops,
sift plastic for gold.

*

The book lies face-down,
we've lost our place, the speech
learned by rote but never made.
Not worth the paper on which it's printed
when there are Trees to Save.
Chuck it on the fire,
we'll need its blast of heat
when refineries fall into the sea.

The guts of continental bullies
are strung on the loom of hell –
We'll weave a commemorative quilt
to celebrate our freedom.
The warp and weft of doom
will keep us warm.

*

If we are blame, how to fix our faults?

If we are blade, we're deep in love with blood.

If we are brain, we're plagued by tumour.

If we are broken, we're past repair.

If we are bible, we've lost faith.

If we are birth, we're also grave.

If we are bird, we crow for meat.

If we are breath, we've ceased.

*

Through dark open mouths
climbs a sound unrelated to word –
        A quaver that skips the stave,
        quivering on breath.
        The wail of veiled women at a grave.
        The scream of falling Icarus slicing air.

*

The book lies face-down,
keeps its counsel. Pick it up,
or chuck it on the fire. It's been here
for years, collecting dust, the author
long dead.

His time was up

but now he takes another shape,
his voice pressed like a flower in the page,
asking us to speak to him, to bring him
back to life.

Just a matter of time
they say, as if time has mass and weight,
like bricks – we build a wall each day,
demolish it each night, then
build it up again, brick by sodding
brick. Our stocks are made of air
and spit, they black in smog.

*

The thoughtless world ticks off its inventory:

four births two deaths every
second, eight million heartbeats every
second, seventy-five Big Macs every
second, five hundred WhatsApps every
second. Four thousand new stars every
second burst into gravity; we *know*
but can't *see*.

All of it adds up to
one: a belief in what we think is true.

*

In the nick of time they say, a chip
off the clock, what happens
before what might have happened –
disaster halted, or simply held
for another day.

                Your time is up.

*

The storm grabs what it can –
gated estates jerry-built on fault lines,
makeshift hospitals, highways
carved into crazy paving.

The host of daffs break ground
for Christmas, the blackbird sings
all night, hypnotised by LEDs.

*

The book lies face-down, an open fan,
a cabbage white, or so the poet said:
everywhere, nowhere, vanishing from sight.

His tomb is laced with praise,
his slim volumes are what remain,
cluttering glum shelves.

The book lies face-down. Pick it up.
Text riddles the page, fencing the pure
white field with strokes.

They say the poet spouts a lot of
rubbish: things that are like things,
instead of things that just are.

Things have volume, occupy space.
Words balloon over our heads,
pop in the stifling air.

                    Full   stop.

*

If we are blood, we're clot.

If we are blue, we're bruise.

If we are bile, we're humour.

If we are bind, we're tied together.

If we are bread, we're mould.

If we are blench, we cheat.

If we are billion, we'll increase.

If we are breath, we've ceased.

            *

No more boom, just bust.
No more room, go home.
No more hands across the channel
once we dynamite the tunnel,
clinging onto inflatable dinghies,
reliving Dunkirk pluck.

No more odes, just prose.
No more love, just lust.
No more meat, less protein –
no sitting when we must stand.

No more time. We've run out,
as if time is a tarmacked road
that simply ends – what's ahead
is unmade.
                        Better to stay
confined inside our crumbling
palace to seethe and rot alone.

No more milk and honey,
just flat beer. Get used to it.
The storm is here.

Artwork Captions

All works by Robert Rauschenberg. Reproduced by kind permission of the Robert Rauschenberg Foundation.

p35 *Canyon*, 1959. Combine: oil, pencil, paper, fabric, metal, cardboard box, printed paper, printed reproductions, photograph, wood, paint tube, and mirror on canvas with oil on taxidermied golden eagle, string, and pillow. 81¾ × 70 × 24 in (207.6 × 177.8 × 61 cm). The Museum of Modern Art, New York. Gift of the family of Ileana Sonnabend.

p37 *Rhyme*, 1956. Combine: oil, fabric, necktie, paper, enamel, graphite, and synthetic polymer paint on canvas. 48¼ × 41⅛ in (122.6 × 104.5 cm). The Museum of Modern Art, New York. Fractional and promised gift of Agnes Gund in honor of Richard E. Oldenburg.

p39 *Hymnal*, 1955. Combine: oil, paper, fabric, printed paper, printed reproductions, and wood on fabric with telephone directory, metal bolt, and string. 64 × 49½ × 7¼ in (162.6 × 125.7 × 18.4 cm). Private collection.

p41 *Monogram*, 1955–59. Combine: oil, paper, fabric, printed paper, printed reproductions, metal, wood, rubber shoe heel, and tennis ball on canvas with oil and rubber tire on Angora goat on wood platform mounted on four casters. 42 × 63¼ × 64½ in (106.7 × 160.7 × 163.8 cm). Moderna Museet, Stockholm. Purchase 1965 with contribution from The Friends of Moderna Museet (The Museum of Our Wishes).

p43 *Bed*, 1955. Combine: oil and graphite on pillow, quilt, and sheet, mounted on wood support. 75¼ × 31½ × 8 in (191.1 × 80 × 20.3 cm). The Museum of Modern Art, New Yor. Gift of Leo Castelli in honor of Alfred H. Barr, Jr.

p45 (left) *Factum I*, 1957. Combine: oil, ink, graphite, crayon, paper, fabric, newsprint, printed reproductions, and printed paper on canvas. 61¼ × 35⅞ in (155.5 × 91 cm). The Museum of Contemporary Art, Los Angeles. The Panza Collection.

(right) *Factum II*, 1957. Combine: oil, ink, graphite, crayon, paper, fabric, newsprint, printed reproductions, and printed paper on canvas. 61⅜ × 35¾ in (156 × 90.7 cm). The Museum of Modern Art, New York. Purchase and an anonymous gift and Louise Reinhardt Smith Bequest (both by exchange).

p47 *Trophy I (for Merce Cunningham)*, 1959. Combine: oil, graphite, metallic paint, paper, fabric, wood, metal, newsprint, printed reproductions, and photograph on canvas. 66 × 41 × 2 in (167.6 × 104.1 × 5.1 cm). Kunsthaus Zürich, Switzerland.

p49 *Trophy IV (for John Cage)*, 1961. Combine: metal, fabric, leather boot, wood, and tire tread on wood, with chain and flashlight. 33 × 82 × 21 in (83.8 × 208.3 × 53.3 cm). San Francisco Museum of Modern Art. Purchase through a gift of Phyllis C. Wattis.

p51 *Levee*, 1955. Combine: oil, paper, printed paper, printed reproductions, fabric and necktie on canvas. 55 × 42¾ in (139.7 × 108.6 cm). Private collection.

p53 *Trophy V (for Jasper Johns)*, 1962. Combine: oil, fabric, cardboard box, printed paper, plastic ruler, and metal-frame window on canvas. 78 × 72 × 7½ in (198.1 × 182.9 × 19.1 cm). Honolulu Museum of Art. Gift of Mr. and Mrs. Frederick R. Weisman in honor of James W. Foster, 1971 (4022.1).

p55 *Summerstorm*, 1959. Combine: oil, graphite, paper, printed reproductions, wood, fabric, necktie, and metal zipper on canvas. 79 × 63 × 2½ in (200.7 × 160 × 6.4 cm). Michael and Judy Ovitz Collection, Los Angeles.

p57 *Painting with Grey Wing*, 1959. Combine: oil, printed reproductions, unpainted paint-by-number board, typed print on paper, photographs, fabric, stuffed bird wing, and dime on canvas. 31 × 21 × 2½ in (78.7 × 53.3 × 6.4 cm). The Museum of Contemporary Art, Los Angeles. The Panza Collection.

Notes

'Blue Rag Zine' is a cut up of 'Gaberlunzie' by Douglas Dunn.

The vertical texts in 'Field Companions' are taken from two texts by John Cage: *Music Lovers' Field Companion* (1954) and *Mushroom Book* (1972).

'Coyote in the Suburbs' references a 1974 performance by the artist Joseph Beuys titled 'I Like America and America Likes Me', where the artist spent three days living in a single room with a live coyote.

Night opened in me an inn for phantoms is a paraphrase of a statement from Gaston Bachelard's *La poétique de la reverie* (1960).

The 'Combines' poems are based on a series of hybrid works made by the American artist Robert Rauschenberg between 1954 and 1964, bringing together painting and collage with an assemblage of cast-off objects. Rauschenberg said he wanted to incorporate things he couldn't make himself to create an element of surprise; he talked about working 'in the gap between art and life.' It was Rauschenberg's fellow artist and lover Jasper Johns who coined the term 'combines' and he makes an appearance in my sequence, along with John Cage, Merce Cunningham and Cy Twombly. The final poem in the sequence, 'Painting with Grey Wing' quotes a line from the Frank O'Hara poem 'For Bob Rauschenberg'.

'In Memory' is inspired by Jason Farago's *New York Times* piece 'How a Grey Painting Can Break Your Heart', which focuses on Jasper Johns's painting 'In Memory of My Feelings' (1961), which in turn takes its title from a poem by Frank O'Hara.

'Belief Systems' was written as a response to the exhibition *The Bard: William Blake at Flat Time House* which displayed illustrations Blake made in 1797 for 'The Bard' and 'The Fatal Sisters' by Thomas Gray. Gray's work was a revelation for Blake, and through this commission he saw a way to begin to create his own complex illustrated poem cycles. Flat Time House was the home of the artist John Latham, who, like Blake, developed a total world view that shaped his artistic practice and he considered FTHo 'a living sculpture'. The poem stitches together phrases from Blake, Gray and Latham but is also situated in the moment of the poem's birth in February 2020 when Storm Brendan was on the horizon. On my way back to Peckham Rye (where Blake had a vision of an angel) I saw homeless men huddled in the passages outside the station, and a connection formed between their bowed figures and the figure of Blake's Bard. It seems appropriate that these random sightings came together, considering Latham's idea that every occurrence is an 'event' and that all events happen simultaneously, hence the concept of 'flat time.'

Acknowledgements

Some of these poems have appeared in the following print and online journals: *Ambit, Bad Lillies, Black Iris, Cofferdam, Finished Creatures, 14 Magazine, The Robert Graves Review, Long Poem Magazine, Magma, Molly Bloom, Poetry Wales, Raceme, Reliquiae, Shearsman, The Spectator, The Poetry Review* and *Wild Court*.

'The Sea, No. 4' was included in the anthology *All Becomes Art: Part One* (Speculative Books, 2021). 'New Year' appeared in the anthology *After Sylvia: Poems and Essays in Celebration of Sylvia Plath* (Nine Arches, 2022).

'Belief Systems' was commissioned by Chris McCabe and Gareth Bell-Jones for the exhibition *The Bard: William Blake at Flat Time House* in 2020.

'Ignition' is informed by Sara Haq's series of drawings 'Things I did that nobody noticed (but that changed everything)' included in her exhibition *metaphysical conundrums* at Bethlem Gallery in 2021.

The 'Field Companions' sequence was written to accompany Alison Gill's sculptural installation 'Field Magic Commune', as part of the exhibition *A Fine Day for Seeing* at Southwark Park Galleries in 2021.

'Coyote in the Suburbs' was commissioned by Earthsong, a collaboration between Poets for the Planet and Imperial College London and was livestreamed at the UN Climate Change Conference (COP26) in Glasgow in 2021.

'Chirophobia', 'The Killer's Hands' and *Night opened in me an inn for phantoms*' were written to accompany work by sculptor Poppy Whatmore for the exhibition *A Body A Part* at the APT Gallery in 2023.

'Night held' was commissioned by the artist Graham Crowley for his book *Dark Matter*, to accompany the exhibition *Light Fiction* at domobaal in 2024.

My sincere thanks to the Robert Rauschenberg Foundation for allowing me use of the images that accompany the *Combines* poems.

And my gratitude, as always, to my workshop comrades Anne Berkeley, Claire Crowther, Rhona McAdam and Sue Rose, and to Jacqueline Saphra for her friendship and support.